UNSCRIPTED THOUGHTS

DOES YOUR PERCEPTIONS HAVE RESTRICTIONS AS WELL?

PRANJAL KALITA

ISBN 979-888629115-5

This book is dedicated to my late mother, my father, to my distant sister Saraswati who showers me with knowledge and my mentor Shiv ji. I thank my 'Maa' for the love and care that she has always showered me with. I thank my 'Baba' for providing me with enough strength to overcome all the difficulties that life has to offer. I am blessed to have a sister who has shown me the path to one's knowledge and lastly I also thank my mentor Shiv ji who has guided me by showing the right path throughout my life.

Contents

Contents

Disclaimar

This book is clearly a representation of the author's thoughts and observations. In no way does this book insults any individuals thoughts and observations. It clealry respects the thoughts that others have. It is basically an observations and should not be taken too seriously.

Preface

The sole purpose of the book ' 'UNSCRIPTED THOUGHTS' is an effort to put the thoughts and the emotions, that are often neglacted by us in our day to day busy schedule. It is an observation by the author related to hidden meanings that he has with different aspects of this world.

CHAPTER ONE

THE NATURE SPEAKS.

Nature is anything that surrounds the environment, whether it is plants, animals, air, water, fire, sand, rocks, soil, insects etc. Everything is nature. Every single little thing that nature has provided us, has a hidden message for everyone of us.

Look at the sun, it provides us the heat that we need and protects us from getting cold, and sends us a hidden message *to protect* everyone in their difficult times. The Rain drops that falls from the sky tells us that *tears* will be there in everyone's lives but it will also *get vanished* after sometime, the fire helps us in cooking food to providing us warmth and sends us a hidden message *to feed* the ones that doesn't have food to *eat* and *a place to sleep*. The Lightning and the thunder guides us *to overcome fear* at any point of our life, the strong winds asks us to remain *strong* and move *forward* in life's difficult times. *Time* sets up a remainder, that everything is *temporary*, sunrise is like *the beginnings or happiness* while sunsets is like the *endings or the sorrows*. Plants provides us with the oxygen that we need and in return we provide them with carbon dioxide, which means that, *life is all about sharing and caring.* The *unity* to fight against the odds can be seen in the wild, which guides every humans that *unity is the ultimate strength.* The sky and the uneven clouds tells us that *knowledge* and *creativity are endless.*

Almost everything on nature has an indirect way of sending a message to us. The different *visionary* pictures and images, that we can imagine within the clouds speaks us how artistic and creative, our thoughts can be.

Have you ever look at a spider and notice about the fact, that the insect stays in the same place for hours to days to even months? This little gift of nature tells us to *be patient and remain calm* throughout our life. An ant remains busy in every part of its life, which sends us a message to remain *busy* by *being a workaholic* and never stop doing hard work in any point of our lives. The Rats are able to find their foods in any difficult place they live in and fights for its freedom if gets caught and sometimes wins too which basically means we can *get out of our poverty if we try,* and even if we face difficulty in it we could still *be the one coming out victorious.* Cows provides us milk which tell us *to share the things that we have,* horses tells us that you can be *strong* and at the same time be *humble too.* The *ups and downs* that we have in our life can be compared to the hills and the plateaus. The *height* of the Mountains tells us how *far* we can go, where we *stand now.* The mighty rivers can hold the *music of your thoughts and emotions.*

The different smell and colours that each beautiful flowers has, sends us a hidden message that every human is *different* in terms of colour of their skin to religion to culture and yet so beautiful and the list of the nature goes on and on.

What comes to your mind when you think about God? To most it will be religion as religion educates and directs us about God. Question emerges have you at any point seen the all-powerful in the outright structure? Have you at any point communicate with him in genuine? All things considered, we realize we as a whole have our responses. Direct communication with the almighty, is beyond the realm of possibilities, when we are bended with materialistic necessities and wants. To understand the consciousness, we have to first liberated ourselves from the unconsciousness that we carry alongside us. There have been different sages and yogis living in and around the Himalayas, who have reached their consciousness and truly understands the sole reason for life, such mentionable names are Maha avatar Babaji, Lahiri Mahasaya, Swami Sri Yukteswar Giri, Paramahansa Yogananda, Haidakhan Babaji,Rama Krishna Paramhansa, Maa Anand Maya, Neeb Karori Baba and others.

Every little thing that is there in the Nature is created by the Creater, which means every part of the Nature represents God.

Almost everything on nature has an indirect way of sending us a message, this is the ultimate gift of nature that it sends us and yet we are unaware of.

CHAPTER TWO

THE PLEASURES ARE DOPAMINE

On the off chance, that you were given a decision, to pick either watching a film or to read a book for two to three hours? What will be your decision? For the vast majority of us, it will be to watch a film. We should circle back to an another decision, assume you were going to pick between a rundown of things like watching a web series, eating your scrumptious quick food varieties, doing shopping, listening to your cherished music, purchasing a branded phone, playing your beloved computer games, surfing your web-based media profiles, watching funny videos and on the opposite side of the rundown, things incorporates, for example, reading a book for a couple of hours, doing exercise, doing contemplations, cleaning your garments, washing your dishes and utensils, eating fresh foods rather than branded junk foods, which side will you like to accomplish more?

We realize we have our responses, we will like to do the things that gives us a more pleasures and satisfaction rather than things which will assist us with developing and make progress, it is a direct result of a substance that is in our brain which is known as **'dopamine'**, it is a synapse which gives you fulfilment joy, pleasure and satisfaction, it is additionally called as the *'blissful chemical or the happy hormone '*. Dopamine nearly controls all aspects of you and consistently searches for things, that gives you instant prizes and delights with practically zero efforts, than things that gives you less pleasures with more efforts.

All the different pleasures that we craved for are nothing but dopamine. We usually love to eat foods that are delicious and unhealthy rather than foods that are non delicious but healthy, we love those foods because as soon we eat them it creates a dopamine inside our brain, the more taste the food has the more dopamine we get , we feel a sense of satisfaction and pleasure while eating delicious foods, you may find people in their youth having flirtations with someone who they are attracted to, this is because the flirtations creates a dopamine in their brain which gives a sense of pleasure to a particular individual, we do spend most of our time scrolling social media accounts to pages, watching short videos, looking for memes by spending hours in it, we are addicted to these stuffs, because we instantly receiving happiness and satisfaction by surfing in the internet, because we are constantly receiving enough dopamine by doing such things.

Dopamine is not completely bad, as it also motivates us in doing something that we love and that is good as well, but the modern companies have studied and have tried to create and give us an environment or a product through which we receive more and more dopamine and have less gains too, for example when we upload a content such as a new profile picture on our social media profiles, after a few seconds notifications started to pop up on our screen, we engage into that two or three minutes to see who has like our image, we want to see the reactions, we want to see who commented on our picture, what is his thoughts for our picture, these instant reactions makes us happy because our brain immediately generates dopamine at that time.

When we study it takes efforts to complete a chapter and we feel tired on moving onto the next chapter but if we assume to watch a decent web series, we can finish every one of the episodes without having a break or without eating something, this is a direct result of the consistent and significant degree of dopamine we get by watching every episodes to every seasons as compared in getting less dopamine by completing a chapter of a book.

There are people who have a regular habit in smoking, drinking liquor and even illicit drugs, they realize that these substances are terrible for their health but they take them consistently, they are dependent on this, because it helps them to get high dopamine through this substances, dopamine is the powerhouse of all addictions, it gives you motivation to do anything that you love and get satisfactions and pleasures, it is not a bad thing or a good thing, but the problem is we indulge and gets addicted to things which are not beneficial to us. If we shut down the things that are not beneficial and do things that are beneficial for us such as doing exercise, studying, reading, learning a new skill, doing things which are passionate too and are good for us we can still get dopamine from them, starting from low to high.

Now we will learn about, how to restrict and control ourselves from things which gives us high levels of dopamine and are not beneficial for us. For this we need to comprehend and apply the dopamine detox. Dopamine detox is an interaction through which an individual maintains a strategic distance from dopamine delight triggers for a specific timeframe.

Presently let us talk about how can you apply the dopamine detox? You have to do nothing, but simply avoid all sort of things from which gives you pleasures and satisfaction, for a single day. You have to avoid all those things which give more dopamine instantly in a split second like listening to music, playing computer games, surfing your web-based media profiles, watching funny videos, sitting in front of the TV, eating anything scrumptious, having a call with an extraordinary companion, watching a web series and also the things which gives you less dopamine with more efforts, like doing exercise, sleeping, reading books, cooking, doing specific works of your home.

Basically you have to do absolutely nothing for a day, you can drink water, you can sit, you can walk to a distance on the off chance that you feel to exhausted, the walk should be exceptionally limited to a distance, you should avoid even communication with your friends in real too, you have to completely make your day boring for a single day. When you wake up, in the next day, you need to totally disregard and keep away from the things that gives you high dopamine with less efforts, which are not really great for you, you need to do the things that gives you less dopamine and are advantageous for you like reading, working out, learning a new skill, doing contemplation, eating healthy.

Enjoying this consistently for a month and try to keep away from the things through which you get more dopamines, but remember that your brain controls you to a great extend, it will always manipulate you into doing things that gives you instant pleasures and if you didn't try to avoid the thoughts of your mind, it will again take you back to the old stage.

At the very beginning, it will be a bit hard for you since you have already made an habit of getting high dopamine every day, it will be excessively challenging for yourself and you can get push down of not getting higher dopamine, that you once had, so try to take less amount of higher level dopamine like instead of watching a full web series, just resist yourself with one episode a day, instead of surfing your phone for six hours, limit yourself to an hour a day.

Spend your day by doing productive things, like studying for few hours, doing exercise and yoga, doing meditations, cleaning your clothes, washing your dishes and utensils, eating fresh fruits. You can also set a reward for yourself, when you complete a less dopamine and productive level work. Like if you have completed a chapter of any subject then after completion, reward yourself by doing things that you love, it can be anything but it should be for a limited period.

You will be bored in the initial stage, but advancing day after day, you will find that it actually works at the end. By engaging in qualitative works for more and more you will get higher dopamine in productive works too and lesser dopamine in less productive works and that phase your physical and emotional state will be directly controlled by you.

CHAPTER THREE

SEEKING AND GRANTING FORGIVENESS

Almost every single one of us had done something wrong with others at some point of our life. We never realised how our actions and words can curse or hurt others even if we don't want it to be, we loose control of our senses and later realised our fault, we become shameful for our actions, we lament from our past, later we learn from our mistakes and get a legitimate vision about good and bad, and thus, we look for forgiveness.

On the contrary similar situations happens to us, where something awful happens to us, we have to decide whether to forgive someone or not. This is the moment, where we have *a choice* to *grant forgiveness.*

Seeking and granting forgiveness to others are almost same, if we analyse it in depth.

Allow us first to comprehend on seeking someone for forgiveness. Presently prior to understanding the Why perspective let us comprehend the **'Who'** angle first. Who generally seeks others for forgiveness? A person who realise about his mistakes, a person who can judge himself as wrong, a person who understands the value of the other person and most importantly a person who can let go of their ego, can seek others for forgiveness. When someone says 'sorry' it also means that the person is letting himself down upon others, not because someone has forced him to do so, but he himself thought of bowing down to someone because he realises his faults.

Most people *cannot seek forgiveness* or doesn't want to because they cannot think themselves as wrong or doesn't have any desire to, in light of the fact that they can't think themselves as off-base, they always think themselves as right in every manner, they never can see their missteps regardless of whether they won't relinquish their self image, they doesn't have the mindset to bow down to others as they have a *solid confusion* of reasoning themselves *right on each angle.*

Now lets come to the **'why'** aspect of seeking forgiveness, Why do we need to seek forgiveness from others? It can be n number of reasons, like we may now realised that we were wrong, at some point of our time, we may realise our mistakes, we want to make the negative roads to the positive turns, in short we want to correct ourselves and let go off the ego and try to make things clear once again.

Drawing closer to the next part, let us understand *why we should grant forgiveness.* First, we really want to comprehend here that, in this very scenario, we are the one who got hit by somebody, when somebody harms us bad, we have a natural characteristic inclination of disliking the individual, it's totally ok, we have our own arrangement of feelings for ourselves and for others. When someone tries to seek forgiveness from us, our egos and self esteem were at its pinnacle, we judge them too quick, too casually without acknowledging, about the fact that, we are also playing the role of them in someone else story. When someone apologize for their mistakes, *they understands our torments, they regrets and in order to rectify their wrong doings, they apologize, they want us to heal but because of our egoistic mentality,* we couldn't forgive them. We couldn't and don't want to forgive them which also means that here we are nothing but like a kind of God for them in this context, where we can heal them by *granting forgiveness* but we *refuse to heel do so* because we are *not matured enough to forgive others.*

And once we cannot forgive others, we at the same time *should also not desire* to *receive forgiveness* from others. Indeed, even how hard the past was we can give up off the past and start a new beginning but we choose not to. We also want others to suffer and want to see others placed below us, these are the thoughts which we indirectly possess, but didn't want to say. *We should put an end to the wrong thoughts of a person, not the person itself.* When we don't have the mentality of *granting forgiveness,* we *should also not have a false desire* of *receiving forgiveness from God.*

Think of the misunderstanding the miscommunication that we have with our parents. Think about your siblings, do they seek forgiveness? Yes they do. Do we grant forgiveness? Yes, we do. Why it is a certain answer? Because here ego takes a back seat, hatred cannot be there for family, which means we can *seek and forgive anyone* we want. Only difference is the *choice* and the ability to *think differently* and to see the *unseen side of someone else story too.*

Forgiveness is a choice rather than an option.

CHAPTER FOUR

LOOK INTO THE WORLD AS IF YOU WERE IN YOUR SEVENTIES

Age is all about **experience**, aged people have the best advice with them, they are matured people who have seen the whole experience of life. We know, but we don't try to understand them. How does a person look into the world when they were in their seventies? What would be his dreams? What do they really want in that time of their life? Unlike you, they cannot imagine having a million dollars or getting a job or getting married or to the weirdest possible, go to some wild parties and do weird stuffs, so that they will have something to talk about when they are old.

What do they really need when they are old? **Only love,** what would an old individual be able to need with the exception of affection? All they need is to *give and get* some affection, presently they would rather not value those materialistic things of getting an extravagant vehicle to purchasing a sophisticated house to getting rich, presently they don't have the energy to battle with others, they can't be envious of others, a large portion of individuals they had battles with were no more. The older individual's companion, which he considers his bestfriend could leave him genuinely and profoundly, at a point in his excursion. A large portion of his companions were nowhere to be seen, presently the main thing he really focuses on is affection, which he hopes to get from his own family, yet his children will be caught up in fighting the battles of the world for getting something *and they will lack the capacity to deal with their folks.*

Presently, this extremely matured individual will totally have an inverse and *different view,* from the perspectives that he once had, when he was youthful. He will understand that each materialistic longings, that he had run for throughout his life has now became less incentive for him, even if someone hands him all the materialistic things that he had once desired, he might immediately rejected them all real quick.

Presently, he would rather not make any foes, he would rather not battle, he would rather not be rich, he doesn't need notoriety, just the only thing he craves for is *love.* May be he wants to make some new friends also, that's why a grandfather and a grandson became friends easily, because those are the two *distinct timings of our life, where we have less materialistic longings.* He will understand that the *time and the energy* that he had spent in running for his materialistic cravings, had set him *back* considerably more which he had acknowledged towards the end part of his life. The *expense is the affection,* that he might have given more to the people that he cherished for, however a lot of his friends and family are no longer with him or had left him long ago.

What we gain from the matured man from his seventies is that, we ought not totally end all our materialistic cravings, since these things also contributes towards our happiness, however should be aware of the fact that, while running for these things, we should invest in some time to enjoy with our family to cherish ones, we should invest in some time to chat with our folks, we can also save a long hourly call with our bestfriends, we can play with our children, we can likewise go with a supper date with our better half every conceivable month even following thirty years of marriage, we can just skip being jealous , we can skip a fight with someone because at the end hatred and enmity towards someone is nothing but unnecessary waste of them for both of us, we can all together with our family can have at least a meal together in a day . *Because at the end, your life is all about your memories and yes memories do matters.*

CHAPTER FIVE

LOVE LETTERS OR SOCIAL MEDIA LOVE?

Have you at any point, paid attention to the good old stories of your parent's generation, when they had been in their twenties having a chai with their soul mate, where love used to be phenomenal from the adoration that we used to have now in our twenties? The qualification in Love today and then became so vast, that it had no other option then to get ruined.

What used to be the situation in those previous days, when our folks age use to be youthful? A boy and a girl seeing each other was such a big thing, as only a few boys and girls were able to get education, where they can actually meet and talk. Having infatuation with any girl or a boy was not so common, as contact with the opposite sex was so much limited and restricted.

Regardless of whether one gets captivated in love, at an early age, admitting the affection was once even a particularly troublesome assignment, explicitly for a young adult, as he needs to contemplate his family's grains, right from an early age with the exception of or beside education. The money related problem in every family used to be at its top during those times, that one ought to scarcely expect about having a profound friendship with someone. However, even without these, there had been a rare sorts of people who got proper education, went into higher colleges, and afterward eventually become hopelessly enamoured.

Regardless of whether one loves somebody, admitting was once a critical step in comparison to the present time, they didn't have any web-based media accounts, where they could undoubtedly track down them and get associated. The arrangement was either to examine straight away or have a common buddy and make them a transporter of your love. However, the present period could without any stretch, enables us to enter the name of our appreciated one, on a search bar, through which we could find them easily and later convey through message.

However, what might be said about the confession for affection? The Older age had likely a couple of ways of communicating their adoration towards someone, out of which, one such way was the **"LOVE LETTER"**. Meeting your lover was once restricted to school, stops, or even film theatres.

Then, what was the basic and the common Non Verbal means of communication? It was those **"letters of love"** written with the tip of the fountain pen for expressing emotions. The letters were covered up and hide in between the pages of notebooks.

There was no limitations of the number of times, that those letters were read repeatedly again and again. More intense the love was, more the amount of perusing it over and over again. But, the present youth cares less, as texts were easily conveyable by means of web-based media, which in this manner prompts less endeavours, where the sentiments became increasingly less, as printed feelings through online media developed to be ethereal, prompting more prominent misperceptions.

However verbal communication today, is more as opposed to the bygone eras. The majority of the dismissal in a relationship, is generally incited in light of misperception through social media whether it is through literary messages, stalking each other profile comment section to stalking each others last seen's, to comparing your love life to others love life, to even erasing your own profile is nothing but a slow poison, which we can refer to as **Social Media Love.**

Relationship separations are normal nowadays, as we are getting everything effortlessly, and we have taken everything for granted. Today the second, you need to transmit a message, you can do it in no flat time. While in the olden times, you need to hang tight for the ensuing gathering or you need to compose and think it twice, prior to putting your into the letters and at the same time focusing on the other individual's sentiments.

Presently, squashing or crushing anybody can be easily performed, with the tip of your fingers without even thinking about the other individual's feelings. This is the harmful reality that we are heading towards. Besides love letters pictures of the significant other was also not easily accessible at that time, where only a single black & white photograph can be accessed and which were later, kept and preserved along with those love letters.

The situation are completely different now, one could easily see various pictures from their web-based media accounts. The feelings towards photos are still there, but the value turned out to be less.

Memories with love letters will be cherished to the deepest core, when the couple will be at their sixties, as they can really relive those moments once again by perusing each letter again and again with a grateful smile on their face. Love social media doesn't have these features as the chats will disappear and even if chats are restored, emotions will be less. How can I even contrast a computerized text with an actual letter?

The solution of this is simple as sound, Try to take Real-life genuinely rather than the reel life. A digital identity can never be real as it is just a replica of you, not the original or the real you.

CHAPTER SIX

RAGES TO RICHES.

The four letter word **'Poor'** teaches us a lot about us specially about the behavioural and hypocritical mindset that we have. We have sympathy for poor people however, we would rather not accompany poor people. We don't welcome poor individuals to our general public, we don't welcome them to our homes regardless of whether they live close by us, most of the malls and big fancy restaurant wouldn't welcome a poor to come in even if they have money. And we call ourselves as civilised people? What kind of civilised people are we? If this is the example of so called civilised people, then we don't want to get civilised. The accommodation that you will get in an unfortunate onc's home will be a lot of prevalent than a rich home.

But, besides this we can accept with specific factors that the poor are a lot more assiduous in correlation with the wealthy in specific parts of life. The unfortunates, fortunately knows the genuine reality of the general public and can without much of a stretch perceive any individual while the rich knows just a specific piece of reality with regards to the general public.

The appetite that an unfortunate will have in accomplishing something will be a lot more grounded than an individual who is rich if gets equivalent or sometimes less opportunities. There are numerous instances of slumdog millionaires, who have come their direction from the spots where there is trouble in occupying a one time legitimate meal to places where they are feeding the families of others.

Oprah Winfrey, the richest black women in the world 2021 didn't had running water and electricity when she was growing up, renowned author J.K Rowling once told her experiences of being a single parent, stopped eating so that her daughter could eat, she told in an interview about the nights when there was literally no money. These are striking internationals instances of individuals who diverted their life from poverty to newfound wealth.

Well, we should check out our own country too, Narayana Murthy, the father of Infosys, had only 20,000 rupees that he took from his better half's savings when he started Infosys, which later on became a billion dollar firm. Late Dhirubhai Ambani, was a gas station attendant who didn't gave up on the idea of doing something big and great founded the reliance industries, which is now one of the biggest multinational companies in India and throughout the world. Kannada Actor, Naveen kumar Gowda otherwise known as Yash, who got his distinction from his blockbuster film KGF once ran off from his home with 300 rupees on his hand, to turn into an actor but little did he knew about acting, he joined theatre which he didn't knew anything about, his income came from behind the stage by selling tea, even in a meeting he told that in the past he used to rest in the roads and now the time has totally changed where a major banner of him, from his film, is there on that same place where he once slept.

Various aspirants have cracked one of the top ranked exams like UPSC, Saffin Hasan who cracked the pioneer exam, dedicated his success to his mother who made thousands of rotis and chapattis in marriage halls in order to fulfil her son's dream. He had slept several days with an empty stomach, M Sivaguru Prabhakaran slept in railway station before he cracked the prestigious exam, Ansar Shaikh, son of rickshaw driver cracked civil services at 21, in his first attempt itself.

What do this people teaches us? *Poverty* has *no relation* with *your aim,* the only thing you need is to believe upon yourself and *built enough confidence* while pursuing your dream. When God doesn't gives you the things that you *crave for,* he *wants you to fight* for the things, once you start to fight, you fall, you get back again, you fight again, you learn through your mistakes and then you finally *get* what you have always wanted. Now, not only you got the thing that you have always wanted, but you also respect and *value* that particular thing. God didn't gave you effectively the things you needed, if he gave you the things with such ease, you could have never figured out how to esteemed those valuable things, which additionally marks up a question as if the rich are actually poorer and the poor are richer. .

CHAPTER SEVEN

THE REAL REASON OF YOUR SADDNESS

Through this section, we will examine about the genuine explanation of your distresses. To discover your distresses, we should take a gander at the things through which you get joy. Above all, where do you get your happiness from? No doubt you get happiness, when you get the things you need or like, such as purchasing your dream car, getting your dream job, talking with your favourite person, tie a love knot with the woman or man you love, getting fame, travelling in your favourite place, buying a sophisticated home, being rich, wearing designer clothes to branded shoes to even having your delicious dish.

Look at the sources of happiness that you desire for, all your happiness comes externally. They are all external. You are *searching* for *happiness outside,* while the *happiness* that you get *occurs inside.* Actually we are not craving for happiness, we are simply *looking and collecting* all sort of things through which we are getting happiness. And when you collects such things, you also generates a fear of losing them. Happiness lies within you, you don't have to seek outside every single day in every different things.

Problems emerges more, if you think such and such people are there, through which you obtain your happiness from. That implies you are allowing your satisfaction to be constrained by an outside energy. Now all of your satisfaction rest in to that particular individual, which additionally implies by the second *you get disconnected from that individual all of joy will be gone real quick*, you will be placed into anxiety and tensions. You are *letting an outer being* control your *inner happiness and satisfaction*. Why are you letting this happen? Just because you cannot forget the person, you once had good memories with? Try *to forget* them, take time but *try to forget*, you should give *zero priority* to such persons who *doesn't adore or value your emotions*, the world has thousands reasons to *smile*, then why keep looking for that one reason to *cry?*

Each of your distresses comes externally from individuals, to materialistic things, to stressful dreams and for that reason you are tragic and stress every single second, that you spent. Simply try to recall the days when you were around five years of age, would you say you were unsettled back then? Are the explanation of your happiness in those days are the very same reasons that you have today? No, in light of the fact that, in those days, you could be happy *without the need of any outside individual*, you didn't associated or connected your happiness with all the *external materialistic things* that the world has to offer. Only thing you crave for, is to run anywhere you want, roam wherever you like, or do anything you like and still had an immense happiness that you don't have with you at the present time. You had a few things back then but your happiness was more in comparison that you have today, which clearly *means that happiness is within you not outside you.* Many people stay alone all their life yet there are happy why?

You can defeat this **sadness** effectively, by figuring yourself *as a driver* who will be driving *a bus* to its *final destination. The driver will find pedestrians, numerous speed breakers, to potholes, to traffic signals to various left and right turns until it reach its final destination. Now here the driver is you, the bus is your brain, the speed breakers are your over thinking and strain, the potholes are your off-base decisions and mix-ups, the pedestrians are all the external things and person through which you generally seek happiness, the traffic guides you the different ways, where you really want to stop or accelerate your mind as well as your thought process and the final destination of your bus is internal happiness;* **the happiness that is within you.** Now the *road* is all yours, *drive safely.* And yeah always *be happy even you don't want to* be. **As most fortunate individuals may not be joyful, but all joyful people are always fortunate.**

CHAPTER EIGHT

HOW OVERSTIMULATION OF SOCIAL MEDIA LEADS TO LOW ATTENTION SPAN & CHANGE IN BEHAVIOURAL THINKING

When was the last time, you have studied for quite a long time with restricted breaks? Most likely, the night prior to a test. That means you can actually study and have maximum concentration when you were receiving fear at its highest level. In any case, what about the other days? Why don't you get any interest to study? Ok let's assume you don't like studies, let's ask a different question, When was the last time you have watch an informational video which has minimum time of an hour? But we know you generally spend hours of time watching videos. Alright let make it excessively simple for you to reply, if social media reels were upto five minutes, will you still be able to watch those reels?

Modern day, Social Media is nothing less than drugs, drugs are substance dependence and addiction while on the other hand web-based media and others are mental addictions and enslavement. From brain scans research of these sorts of addicted individuals, we were able to find out that there is a lack of attention level, emotional intelligence and poor decision making in these individuals. Watching stories, reels, videos are your new reward which is heavily costing you and your precious time, you think these sort of things, as your rewards because you are getting these things with minimal effort as a result it also causing you less ability to focus.

Social Media is the new drug that is being injected to us indirectly. Overstimulation of Social Media helps in releasing more and more **dopamine**, the chemical that makes you feel pleasure, satisfaction and motivation. Often you get depressed and discouraged and look for motivational videos, while watching motivational videos, you were all hyped up and get motivated for a few seconds. But what happens after that? You again get to a similar state where you used to be, these are nothing but releasing of dopamine on your brain while you were watching these motivational videos.

Let's move into the past, where our granddads were at their youth, when there were no televisions, androids and surprisingly a few radios. Then, comes the age of our folks, where there were radios in almost every single home, TV became popular, when we were youthful and then came the time when each of us has our own set of television, radios, headphones , telephones which where later got converted into a single device. In every update, *humans* have decrease and *decrease average attention span.* A recent study had found that the *average attention span* of humans has fallen *from 12 seconds* in 2000 to *8 seconds* today. People generally loose attention span today after 8 seconds and that is also one the reasons why social media reels gets higher percentage of views. We now have a shorter attention span than a Goldfish. We will not able to watch an good informative video, if it is for long durational hours but we will surely watch a three hour movie or spent hours in a week to complete a seasons of our favourite web series, because the only thing we have been targeted by these big companies is to get insert high amount of dopamine in our brain.

Today, we all know many of the big social media giants hire engineers called **'attention engineers'** who try to make these platforms *as addictive* as possible. All these engineers are not someone who is illiterate, they are all high skilled educated people who were once a topper of some renowned university, they have big ideas, brains and plans. But where do they utilise their ideas? By doing all short of things that degrades humanity. They are producing every evil ideas possible and inserting it to us. This is also what too much of development and education had lead us too. *Real villains are the ones, whom we idolise and see them as heroes.*

Whenever we were discouraged or stress we switch to our cell phones as though as if it is a **depression killer**, no it isn't, rather it is a **depression inserter**. We don't simply click a photo, we clicked thousands of it, selects a few out of those thousands, edit five out of those and upload one out of the best.

Why do we do such things? Because, we care a lot about others views and opinions towards us. We make ourselves completely fake, in order to impress others. We instantly check who commented on our picture, how many views we have got, how many likes we have received, whether our crush had commented or not. Following become less once we get our blue tick. Why? Stop doing this, this is bullshit.

The only individuals that matters are the people who will remain behind your grave, once you leave this very planet. Higher *discouragement* are caused to individuals, *who do web-based media regularly* than who doesn't. We always tend to post only the best memories that we have in our life but do we post the recollections when we got admonish, thrashed, got offended, got dismissed? No, right? But these things happens to everybody. We share our pictures, when we are in a relationship, at the same time individuals who doesn't have a partner, gets discouraged by seeing our love life, they have their deception that everybody is having a sound relationship which isn't the genuine case, because after a few months or years, if you glance back at those profiles, you will view that as a large portion of the photos were either erased or are replaced by a new partner.

Frequently, you will observe individuals of our folks age, spamming your inbox by wishing ' *Good Morning to Good Night'* textual quotation pictures, they were also infected by this mentality of texting someone. Texting someone with a modern phone is like an achievement in their mind. Assuming, that an individual can spare some time, by downloading pictures of wishes and later forward and send it to you and others, why don't the same individual call you and wish you every day? *Don't you think a call will be a better option than a picture which nobody cares about and at last gets erased whenever it is seen?*

Whenever we get our *free time*, we should have spend time with our family, talk with them, which would have *eventually created memorable memories* or if we are so tired to do that, we should have walk round the street at least, to see the tress, birds, animals or to do an exercise, that would have kept us fit or even learn a new skill. But what do we really do and gain in the internet? We spend *limitless and countable hours* on social media, through which we *get nothing.* **We have an input of hundred percent and an output of zero.** Even watching informative videos has a lower output, but what output do you get every day by seeing status, reels, short videos to endless text through social media? We all know, we *love to meet our friends* in schools and colleges *rather than a device,* yet we do the complete *opposite.* **We are intelligent and at the same time a fool too.**

CHAPTER NINE

WHY LOVE IS THE MOST POWERFUL AND THE WEAKEST THING A HUMAN CAN EVER HAVE?

What is love? There is no definite or proper explanation for love, except we can say that adoration is only a blend of *friendship* with the sole viewpoint of satisfaction of one another's cravings. The longings can be emotional as well as physical. In simple words, Love is only a solid bondage of companionship or friendship between any two people, no matter what their orientation is. In single word, love is *friendship* while being in a relationship, don't complicate the term by calling it as the fulfilment of the gap of a partner in your life. Love is additionally about compromising. Love isn't all out captivation towards an individual, fascination is the attraction towards an individual due to his/her outside appearance, fame or popularity. Ultimate result of having infatuation can end in affection, however the beginning stage of fascination can't be named as love.

There are various types of affection:

Eros : Love which happens due to captivation and fascination and accomplished for actual joys and desires.

Pragma : It is the sort of adoration which is based on responsibilities and interests. It is a matured love, that has suffered for a really long time.

Capacity: Love which occurs among guardians and youngsters.

Agape : A mentality of affection towards oneself and everybody anybody in regards to whether with companions or foes.

Philia: Love which happens when you are somewhere down in evident companionships.

Craziness: Obsessiveness over an affection accomplice.

Ludus: Flirting and early phase of close and passionate love.

By and large, *Eros and ludus* gets changed over into *pragma,* in the later phase of adoration.

LOVE TOWARDS YOUR PARTNER

The most important thing that needs to be when you are in love is *"friendship"*. Yes, friendship is the most important factor in love, but why? Allow us, to get it to you extremely speedy and straight forward to you. When you get into a relationship, for what reason do you think yourself as boyfriend and girlfriend? Or on the other hand a couple? Why do you become so possessive about your partner?

Why he or she gets restricted in doing this or that? Why do you put restrictions at the very first place? Because the foremost attitude that that we generally show while getting into a relationship is "Purchasing the rights and freedom of the other individual". Your mindset is only to rule the other individual, because now friendship doesn't comes at the top of your priority list, it is sitting right at the base, *despite the fact that*, it is this very *friendship* which *was at the beginning*, when you *have known* your partner for the *first time*.

What do you get by controlling the very individual you love? Let them be free, let them decide what they need, let them do anything, that they enjoy. Aren't your partner's likes your likes too?

Also assuming, if you do this shitty possessiveness, because you have inner fear of losing them because someone else can grab them from you. Then, at that point, my dear friend *let them go*. Why do you want to get back a person who doesn't value your trust? You don't owe an individual, just because you love them. Also in the event, if you were having too profound fondness for them, assuming it was your fault or shortcoming, request absolution from them. Assuming, if it was your partner's fault and on the off chance, that you think they have changed themselves for you, forgive them. But, *don't get stuck in* where you know, *you can't continue on*, every individual on earth can move on with time. Be patient, let time wrap up of your work.

There will be a period in each individual's life, when they will have their eyes set only for that special someone, it can be their crush to their girlfriend to boyfriend, and will even think of marrying them. We might think of themselves as the only reason for our happiness. But things might turned out to be different and we might loose them at some point. This is because often we think, of making a connection with someone at some point of our lives, but at the end we realized that, it happens only a few times that to with a few people. However, at the same time we also wish we hadn't let them go as a companion.

LOVE TOWARDS YOUR PARENTS

This is one of the most significant love but it is underestimated, as the present youth usually show less amount of affection towards them .There are different instances of men's leaving their folks in their advanced age, when they required them the most, in light of the fact that, the only family that the son cares now, is his family(here his family means his significant other and his kids), he totally overlooks the way that right from the very first breath to the adult man that he is today is additionally a direct result of the adoration and care from his folks, every little wish that he had once requested was satisfied even with the expense of his folks tears. We should try to show at least, *some measure of affection towards them,* talk with them in their old age, at the very end phases of their life the *only wish they have* is to have *endless talks with you,* try to understand the fact that now your folks are old they don't have the same energy to do something that they once had, they simply need somebody with whom they can shared and talk about their past glories and memories. *Try not to take this adoration from them, they haven't taken away anything that you had once cherished.*

LOVE TOWARDS ONESELF

While looking for adoration outside of us, we totally overlooked the affection that we as of now have within us right from the day when we were born, it's called "**Self love**". It is simply *the affection that we have for us,* it is about respecting the individual that you have become today by the different encounters that you had overcome once in your life.

Self love is beautiful, it *doesn't requires any partner.* It *never gets broken.* When you try to love yourself, you look for the aims and goals that can make you satisfied and fulfilled. You positively accept your failures, you believe that everything is not under your control.

Love also develops more, during the times of your **separation** with someone, in any form.

Why is love in any structure is the most powerful and the most fragile thing a human can ever have?

Anything that you do or achieve in your life that makes you fulfilled and showers you with immense happiness has a secret expectation that you neglect, it is simply the adoration that you have either towards yourself, your family, towards others or even for your nation state that motivates you into accomplishing something, which later makes you strong. Out of affection towards anyone you can accomplish anything and move into more prominent statures.

A mother eats less and feeds more to her son of out of affection. Eating less makes her more powerful not weak. A father works additional hours to bring in more cash, so that one day he could undoubtedly convey the monetary heap of his girl's marriage, a freedom fighter or an army cheerfully offers his life for his country, it makes him and the regiment more powerful not weak.

In any case, each coin has two different sides, a similar *love* that can make an *individual strong*, additionally can make an individual *feeble*. The very child that ate well, when his unfortunate mother was eating less can make him powerless, a similar girl could get feeble when she discovers her father didn't cared about his health and well-being, while working extra hours to earn extra income out of love for her daughter?

The same soldier mother gets frail, when she discovers that she lost her son when he was fighting in a war for his country. What might be the state of the family when they find out that one of their relative, who they were messing around an hour ago, just lost his life in a mishap. Love is a beautiful experience, it builds you up to move forward. But it has a *bitter side* to, when you go deep in love, at the same time your soul tend to have build *insecurities and fear* of getting *detached* from that person and when such insecurities are develop your physcial state might be with you, but your mental aspect will be somewhere in *the future,* let go off the fear and let love be in the present reality only, the love that you *have with you 'today'.*

These are one of those reasons why *love* is the *most powerful and the weakest thing* a human could ever get.

CHAPTER TEN

WHAT DOES METAVERSE MAY EVENTUALLY LEAD US TOO?

METAVERSE comes from the interconnection of two words 'meta' signifies 'past' and verse signifies 'universe'. The term was first coined in the fiction novel 'Snow Crash in 1992'.

Controlling the whole world by a sole power probably won't be an imaginable thought to have but it very well may be conceivable through the virtual world. An individual with his vision of choosing what regulations to execute, what culture to take on, what framework to be followed, what obligation to be taken, what limitations to be given? Furthermore besides this, having a sole force of controlling each human essentially and accordingly transforming the arrangement of for all intents and purposes into reality for the new world.

It very well may be the start of the new world order, where individuals can sit in their lounge chair wearing a VR box and in the end encountering another world with new companions, to new streets to new places. Those companions may not always be humans, as it can be a robot too The base will be to accomplish everything through a computer generated virtual reality box.

What currently is more essential to us is examining the advantages and disadvantages about the new virtual world.

The initial period of the meta verse, may lead to anything like strolling in the roads of your area to going on a trip into a far off country and getting back to your country, could be done easily. Going to the concerts of a famous celebrity can be easily done by putting in those set of VR lenses. Taking part and playing global tournaments of your favourite sport might be conceivable. Purchasing digital lands, beloved garments through a shopping centre might be done easily, and afterwards getting them packed and conveyed right behind your real home's doorstep, might be a possibility.

Having a digital relationship with a robot could even take place. Not only this, having a wedding in the meta verse world, to letting your expired love ones to join in digitally and showering you with blessings is even conceivable, as such circumstance has occurred where a youthful couple from Tamil Nadu, India had facilitated their wedding after-party in February, 2022 in the digital world, where the host had Hogwarts (a wizarding school taken from a famous novel) as their wedding subject.

Now let us examine the vital cons that the new world might offer us. First the entire world would be *lackadaisicial*. Lethargy might reach to its most elevated pinnacle. Genuine occasions will be procrastinated. The dependence on the meta verse world, might be so high, to that extent that things which are easy to do today might be the toughest in the future. Going to a shopping centre, to watching films in the theatres, to eating your beloved food sources on a bistro, to working in your office, to playing an ideal game on the playground, to meddling stuffs with your circle in real would either be insignificant or get end. While obtaining the highest level of comfort, men could bear the greatest cost of 'reality'. The sole presence of you may be *switched off.*

The later or last phase of meta verse may be such where VR box might get replaced with VR glasses.

People might forget every real aspects of nature, by being a solitary room sucker. *Preparing your food* may be the *toughest task* for you to do. Going to the next room of your house, may be an immense assignment for you. But at the same time there are sure things which are not even imaginable in the meta verse world like learning swimming. Certain professions like specialists, surgeons, doctors, researchers, mechanics etc are not even possible in the virtual world. People may not be anything other than a virtual robot.

More the time you spend on the virtual world *the less* you experience this *present reality.* The rest of the world's political system may have less worth and could even have an issue of presence. Digital currencies might be the new money. *It will in any case, be a secret to us what fortunate or unfortunate the meta verse or the future world has made arrangements for us?*

CHAPTER ELEVEN

RECOVERING STRESS AND DOING NOTHING IS ALSO A WORK OF DOING EVERYTHING

What is work? Anything which requires *exertion*.What is stress? A psychological strain that an individual goes through to a genuine or envisioned occasion or change by which the individual shows apathy toward his every day exercises. Will you consider stress as work? To answer this question, we need to initially stop accepting work as a exertion of accomplishing something, where the result can been seen practically. A specific event can happen to any individual, where the person goes through stress regularly and do literally nothing, here everyone would have the idea that he had waste a lot of his precious time, no he hasn't. The individual has done a hell of a work, that he could ever think of, he has battled every minute of his emotional pain and his stressful life, *he hasn't blamed any outsider for his circumstances, rather he blames himself for some unacceptable decisions that he made, he realised what is wrong for him and what is right, things are now way lot easier for him to comprehend and with time he defeats every last inch of stress that he once had.* Presently, he doesn't rehashes the misstep that he once made, he is very much aware of his decisions, now he also advices others, when he finds others undergoing the same situations, that he once had.

Stress has become a part of everybody's life nowadays, a father and a mother takes stress for their family, a businessmen takes stress for his money, a patient takes stress for his disease, someone takes stress of the circumstance of his past, someone takes stress for their future, nearly everybody goes through pressure and stress. Some meditates to recuperate from pressure and try to remain calm in stress.

The common view point in stress is that it ends but takes time. But stress is definitely a situation where you think the event should never happen or should have changed, now if the event that should never happen has happened then why on earth are you taking stress? Ask yourself can stress help your mind recover out from stress itself? Ask yourself, is stress the reason of the disturbance that you have on your mind? Ask yourself can stress help your mind recover out from stress itself?

Whenever we take more stress, we keeping going deeper and deeper into it, we over think events to that limit that has nothing to do with reality and at the end we disregard the current reality.

There are two methods for managing stress, first *ponder the event*, that is *causing you stress*, find out *whether it can be addressed or not*, in the event that it tends to *be settled*, try to tackled the issue and you will be *tranquil* and on the off chance, if the *event has no arrangement*, then *you don't need to take stress* for an *event* that you have *no control with*.

If you observe clearly, everything in the world *is very temporary*, even the *stress that you are having now*, lives are temporary and you are worrying about an event that you have no control with, do you think stressful life is excessively extraordinary? No, if you have no stress in your life, it means you have done nothing in your life. *Stress are the results of the wrong choices that you had made, when you make wrong choices, it also opens your eyes in taking right choices too, do you figure out that satisfaction and joy from any kind, will also get end one day or other?*

Stress is straightforwardly toxic. Can we even highlight a stress where we don't think the result as negative? This *too much negativity in stress* can likewise *misinform us, in neglecting and disregarding* every one of the plausible positive results that could have occur.

Remember that, *Stress isn't an answer* for anything, rather it *is a course* of an *event* that is *natural* to *every creature on earth*. It is just *like a fever that each individual* has, in *various phases of their life* with *various temperatures* and everybody *recovers* from it *within time and again gets infected* with it with a *new strain* or form.

CHAPTER TWELVE

DON'T DISTURB THEM

Often you will find people around you sledging someone just because they are different in some form. We often body shame anyone we know, because we know we have an easy pass to get away with. We never think about the other persons emotions while we body shame, we easily named them as a fatty or a skinny.

You will find people passing vulgar comments on someone because they are jealous of the fact that someone has done something more superior to them. You will always find a neighbour who has a habit of scrutinizing the problems of every single house of their neighbourhood, examining them and passing annoying and disturbing comments to everyone. If you are a girl, you will always find a loafer aunty who has a constant habit of pointing a finger to your parents, about your marriage. There will always be a set of people who will poke you at anything you do, whether it is right or wrong, it doesn't matters to them. The only thing they cares about is to poke you consistently. Many people have been bullied in schools and colleges for fun.

Narcissists generally have the tendency to disturb anyone they like, but to be general no one can disturb us if we don't allow them to. If you think yourself that whatever way, they disturbs you, you will hardly react to it, the only thing that you will do when such people arrives is *to smile* at their face and *then ignore and ignore.* Their so call acts of disturbing your peaceful state can get demolished because you consider them and their words totally useless. If a person has a habit of disturbing you too often for their fun, then don't be close with that person. When you tell them and speaks out about their disturbing behaviour and still they does the same things to annoy you, just leave them even if they are your old mates. By avoiding and ignoring such idiots, you can be a genius.

CHAPTER THIRTEEN

THERE IS NO NEGATIVE WITHOUT A POSITIVE AND NO POSITIVE WITHOUT A NEGATIVE.

Our universe comprises of vibrations and energy whether it is *negative or positive*, same as every little to big thing in the nature too. In case of humans, we have both *negative* and a *positive* energy *within us*, we also do certain things which are good for everyone and do things which are terrible for everyone.

Every person on earth is a reason for *someone's happiness* and *someone's pain* too, which means *the same person* has a *positive* as well as a *negative* personality within him for every different beings, the same person can be rude with someone and at the same time can be soft with someone too. When we make friends, we indirectly look for the people that *matches our energy*, more similar the energy, more close we become. Emotions such as dread, outrage, pitiful, envy and so forth are largely pessimistic energies that we have inside us, though satisfaction, valiance, love, affableness, serenity, sharing and caring to respecting, are the positive energies, that we have within us. A similar individual has both negative and a positive nature of propensities that they develop by being in various environment.

An individual turns out to be positive or negative by the impact of the environment, that he lives in. A person who does a money heist denotes a pessimistic impact to the world, however the money that he had looted might be to save somebody's life is a positive impact to that individual, here we don't support such ideas but we talk about the aspect that every person has a good and an evil side with him, evil side are a result of the darkness that a person faces in his life.

Now let's look into the natural environment too, we all know the importance that rivers and lakes have for us, it provides water for irrigation, provides water for drinking, helps us to develop and generate hydel power, assists in fishing and are rich in providing foods like fish and other aquatic animals. These are all positive aspects that rivers provide us, but the same rivers are also the cause to increase the possibility of flooding thereby causing destructions everywhere, even if a river never floods, flowing water is still destructive to the land over which it passes. The Sun through its sunlight, strengthens your immune system, helps to heat water, dry clothes, helps plants to grow, fights off depression by helping your brain to release a hormone called serotonin , kills bacteria, reduces your blood pressure, improves your sleep by helping your brain to make another hormone called melatonin but the very sunlight though helps our skin make vitamin D, which is required for bone strengthening but unprotected exposure to sun's ultraviolet rays can damage your eyes, skin and immune system, this damage can lead to skin cancer or skin aging. These are some of the *positive and the negative* aspect, that *nature* has for us, which means everything on *earth is balanced.*

You must be familiar with the symbol of *'yin and yang'.* The philosophical meaning of the symbol *'yin and yang'* absolutely guides all of us, that *every matter is built with a positive and a negative side.* The *'yin'* is the *dark swirl* and the *'yang' is the light one,* and each side contains a small portion of a circle of the opposite colour, which means *everything has an opposite side to it.* 'Yin and yang' are not complete alternate extremes but are connected with one another. It accepts that, *universe is made of energies, vibrations and matter* and they all respond distinctively in various situations by being ' *Yin and Yang'.* Through which we can conclude that *everything* on the *entire universe* is built with *positive* and *negative energies.*

CHAPTER FOURTEEN

WEALTH EQUALITY IS WHAT EVERY HUMAN SHOULD DESERVE BUT SHOULD NEVER HAPPEN.

Income or wealth equality means having **equivalent** measure of **money** which prompts equivalent way of life. It is what every human needs, to get equivalent money related advantages, in each part of life, it looks great for the society where everybody is equivalent financially. But is it really good for the society? Is it worth it? Probably not, everyone has their own importance that they needs to provide to this world.

Income or wealth inequality is good for the society to grow, it is beneficial, as it would indirectly give an opportunity to a deprive person to climb up as high as possible in the monetary ladder of the society. Once he moves forward and upwards, he can also guide others like him and help them eradicate inequality. From the rich to the upper and lower middle class to the poor everyone is interdependent with each other. We all need each other directly or indirectly.

If everyone would have been equal monetarily then who would like to work in the factories, who would even like to work as a labour, who will build our houses, who will even be a waiter, a driver to serve others, who will do farming? Forget about these works, no one would even like to work in the middle sector works too. An officier needs help from his staff which is underneath his position, the staff likewise needs assistance from their lower level workers.

There would be no furniture in your homes assuming there were no craftsmen, there would have been no school on the off chance that there were no educators, there would have not been any houses, no appropriate roads, no architectures if there were no labours. Why will a person become labour if everyone becomes financially equal? Why would someone even become an entrepreneur, run a company and sell his product to others? As even if he works hard, he will eventually get the same amount of money that everyone gets without even working. *Innovation might take a downward curve if everything becomes equal.*

No one will like to work hard, think about why do we work so hard? In order to improve our current situation. No one would like to work hard in a monetarily equal society, this is because even if you work hard you will always be in the same position, you will not grow.

Uniformity looks great when our visions are not clear, inequality in income is what makes our society perfect, when we are odd, we have different roles to play in the society, it is through these *different odd roles* that makes all of us quite *even and unique.* The world would have been an exhausting place assuming everyone of us would have been equivalent or perfect.

Income inequality will generate greater productivity, if people are rewarded greatly for their hard work. Bonus and certain kinds of perks are given in order to encourage the employees to work more efficiently. It is a psychological strategy in order to boost them in doing more work for their benefits.

CHAPTER FIFTEEN

'ZERO TO ONE AND ONE TO ZERO IS LIFE'

What does instantly comes to your mind when I say you the word 'ZERO'? Well, I guess nothing or anything that doesn't have any value or even we can simply say it as **no existence**. Again if you were ask, what does comes to your mind when I say you the word **'ONE'?** Well, I guess something or anything that **has a value** or even we can simply say it as something which **has an existence.**

Everything that is there in the universe, that we see today, has a presence, which implies we can allude to it as **'ONE'** and again the **'ONE'** that we have today will one day reach a conclusion and will have no existence which means **'ZERO'**. Let us look at our planet earth, trillions of years prior, Earth had no presence and presently it has an existence of its own and again it will reach a conclusion as well, where it will have no existence, here earth mirrors a thought of **ZERO TO ONE AND AGAIN ONE TO ZERO.**

If we look at every natural to the materialistic things, that earth adopts and have an existence today, will also come to an end, same in case of humans too. We humans think of ourselves as excessively extraordinary, yes we are too an extent, but during the days when there were dinosaurs living on this very planet, not a solitary human was there, which additionally implies that we as **humans** then, at that point, can be instituted as 'ZERO' when the **Earth** was 'ONE'.

Now let's discuss about you as an individual, you might sometimes think that you are too special for everyone, each and every one wants to be with you, everybody wants to be your companion, you are the sharpest, you are wise among the rest, your abilities are awesome, you make the big difference, God created you for something really damn special purpose or even a mission etc and so forth, which basically referring to you about all the illusions that you could possibly have in your mind. Aaah! You may be, but where were you, before you even born?

We know about the fact, that **today you are 'ONE'** but weren't you **'ZERO' before** you even came into this planet? In any case, when you were **'ZERO'**, nearly all the natural things on this planet was going on and on the day when you will again be **'ZERO' from 'ONE'**, everything that is happening today will still be happening, which basically means *every other thing was still happening from millions and millions of years ago, will also happen millions and millions years after your existence.*

Each satisfaction we get is transitory on the grounds, that at last every other pain of ours is temporary, whatever we receive that is positive or negative has a result of **ZERO TO ONE AND AGAIN ONE TO ZERO.** The different joy and the bitterness, that we as a whole have are in the province of **ONE TO ZERO,** so never have an excessive amount of blissful during your great days and never be too miserable in your awful days, as they ultimately has a ultimate result of **'Nothing'** means **'ZERO'**, what we should be more concentrate is that while we are **'ONE'**, we ought to be thankful for everything whether it its positive or negative, fortunate or unfortunate doesn't make any difference, we simply should be appreciative, why? Since, we are here as **'ONE'** for an exceptionally boundless period and this boundless period is proposed to us by GOD to become appreciative not to be dismal, as when we were children we began with **'ONE'** and the day we pass on, we will end in **'ZERO'**, not only we but every little to big thing that has a mere existence will to become **'ZERO'**, just the spans and the time-frame may fluctuates but the structure is same, that is the reason why we can say that **'ZER0 TO ONE AND ONE TO ZERO IS LIFE'**

CHAPTER SIXTEEN

YOU DOESN'T AUTHORIZE TIME, TIME AUTHORIZE YOU.

Did you at any point felt like, wish I had choose this rather than that, things would have been very different at this point. We often make certain decisions today so that the future be in our hands tomorrow, but does all our decisions go as we wants? The answer is both yes and a no. Some decisions do help us and some doesn't. *Time is the best teacher* that *nature* has *given* to *us,* a person may born poor but can conquered the world, in the end part of his life, this teaches us how *time* takes a person from *having nothing to everything,* when we were young each person has to make a choice in his carrier, some people follow their passion and take a risk they believe in themselves and waits and waits and finally gets a recognition, we people used to get in love with someone at an early age and at that particular time we usually think that the partner we are in a relationship with will be our future spouse and after some years we became strangers from couples, this tells us, how time educates us in every moment that *anything can be changed*, we have seen examples of billionaires and millionaires becoming bankrupt, once who used to have loads and loads of money to spent wherever he wants now doesn't have any money to even clear the debts and vice versa.

Many individuals attempt to follow and duplicate others in fields where they are not intrigued and inside the space of years, they understand that had made off-base decisions, this acknowledgement happens due to time.

See yourself as a student and time as a teacher. You will learn to identify the tears of the phony individuals that were around you as friends to relatives to even the general public of the society, it shows us of the envy and the outrage behind those smiley faces, who were miserable because they can never see your happiness, it instructs you that the vast majority of the promises that people makes are misleading, it shows us in our troublesome times who truly remains with you, it shows us how much individuals profess to cherish you and when opportunity arrives they will double-cross you, out of greediness when money is offered how your own people can turned on you or leave you too quick, time shows us the day your bank balance is full even your foes will want to be your side.

With time we get betrayed by our loved ones, we see the genuine side of others, by confronting different tough spots in life from losing your friends and family, to watching the genuine essences of individuals, to observing how deceptive the world and the general public is, time helps us to develop emotionally, sincerely and profoundly, time requests us that we should remain calm even in our though times, many individuals *takes decisions out of anger* and *later laments* for it, time trains us to show restraint, since time will ultimately give you the things that you generally needed, you just need to be just patient.

Time lets us know, that *nothing keeps going forever, not even something that makes you blissful or pitiful*, time makes us aware of the fact that the words of from the mouth are not the same as the words that lies in the stomach, time asks you to be happy in the present and worry nothing about past or future, *because the present that you have today, is also the past from the future, and the present that you have today, is also the future from the past.*

Time *guides us* that you don't know what is in the future, so always do things that you like, you are interested in and that makes you happy because once you turn old, one day you *might lament* of not chatting with somebody, not expressing your actual sentiments, not pardoning somebody, not following your goals, not following your interest and passion, not travelling to the places you love, not being truly happy because you consider your happiness to be to small, not being joyful for the delicious dishes you like to eat, showing less intrigued while taking to a close buddy, as and so forth, *since today you can do these things therefore time is with you,* however one day time will also leave you aside endlessly and you might lament of not doing your desired activities.

CHAPTER SEVENTEEN

THE REASON FOR YOUR FAILURE IS YOUR DREAM.

What is a **dream?** The subconscious visions, that we have when we are asleep or the visions that you consciously think of yourself to have in the near future. What might be your dreams? It can be anything right from becoming an artist, purchasing a car, living in a sophisticated house, marrying your crush to even becoming a great politician, to become famous, to even getting your desired job, becoming rich or it can be anything else.

Let us be exceptionally forthright, an open and try to comprehend about the reality the quantity of people that have accomplished their supposed 'Dreams'. How many are they? Countable in number, but why? If everybody has at least a solitary dream in their life for what reason they don't accomplish that? This is becomes dreams weren't made to be accomplished. Dreams are dreamt everyday whereas *Aims and goals are achieved one day.* Dreams are some sort of illusion and what do we do with illusions? We simply believe that to be genuine and real someday or other and wonder about the sky, doing absolutely nothing. But on the other hand, *goals and aims* are based on engaging *in action*. Yes, if you develop a certain mentality to achieve something at any cost it becomes an 'Aim' of yours, you might miss the target at first but you will end up hitting the bull's eye at the end. When we make an aim, we set different targets which leads us to our final goal. We complete one target after another, which leads us to our final destination and thus the goals that we have set for us eventually gets completed and the aim is thus achieved.

On the contrary, dreams were just dreamt every single day, we do literally nothing and yet we persuade ourselves that one day our fantasies will transform into the real world. This is only misleading oneself. We were doing nothing but only killing the future through our fantasies, these dreams were never accomplished, they are visionless, fundamentally they are erratic.

Let us assume a scenario, where you have a bicycle to go to school but you don't know how to ride the bicycle, so instead of learning it you are wishing or hoping or we can say **'dreaming'** about the fact that one day you will ride your bicycle. But when you have **an aim** that within a month you will be able to ride the bicycle whatsoever, then you will set small sort of goals and targets; like first of all you will attempt to adjust yourself without falling, the following objective you will have is to ride in least rush hour gridlock regions where you can ride smooth and take legitimate turns, you won't accomplish this at once, you will fall, you will get injured some time or another of your training session. However, **one day you won't fall**, because you will learn **to balance yourself** and when we learn, and when we learn **we grow**, *then after accomplishing the task, ask yourself, what made you achieve that?*

The answer is, you have make up your mind and have decided that whatever happens you *won't stop,*you will *proceed* in light of the fact that, you have your *aim set up.*

Aims never promotes procrastination, dreams do. Dreams are more of a fantasy, more of a hope, while on the other hand *aims are a direction towards a goal that are meant to be achieved.*

CHAPTER EIGHTEEN

PRIDE WITH AN EGO ARE THE SUBSTANTIAL LIES.

Pride is essentially an extraordinary joy around one's own accomplishments, this accomplishments can be of any structure be it material, wealth, gifts, intelligence, muscle influence and even a government job. Pride without an ego is a positive methodology, it will continuously assist an individual in developing, without leaving any adverse consequence in the environment. The individual won't just move up in his particular field, but will likewise impact others in a positive manner, however it is by and large the contrary when one's extreme pride is trailed by an imprudent ego, it will continuously be a pessimistic methodology for any individual, it tends to be way deadly and disastrous.

The individual will be so visually impaired in one's accomplishments or achievement that he will see himself as prideful, he will be haughty at little, to easily overlooked details due to climbing a stage forward in life, he will likewise acquire and climb a stage forward to turn into a more self-important more proud individual ever, out of nowhere, the individual whole friend circle will get changed; because now he will develop a negative attitude in keeping some positive friends, relationship will be a greater amount of flaunting, individuals that ought to have been esteemed more will be maintained aside in a separation. Every last delight, that he appears to have assemble now are only a feeling of misleading fulfilment and joy that he feels by thinking himself as far predominant than others through his eyes.

Pretty much, many individuals pride's are currently followed with an egoistic attitude, just like a wonderful young lady or an attractive man could have an egoistic proudness over his/her body, this sort of individuals are so enlightened by their appeal that they neglect to do everything that life really needs them to do, for what reason do you think the different beauty parlours to beauty products have so much value and have a high demand in the market? Because those business are well aware of their target customers, they know most of their customers wants their faces to glow more in compare with others, there is an indirect competition with others, these egoistic proudness over one's body is *temporary* and will soon *fade away* within *time*, this is thing that they know, but are not concerned with. Such people usually don't have any goals the only way they are conscious of is their physical appearance, on the contrary to which we would like to saythat *beauty with brains are there but rare.*

Same applies for the adolescent's today, exceptionally guys who join gyms not to be sound and fit but rather to post an image of their abs on a web-based media to flaunt, still the majority might contradict the assertion and have a contention that the youth really focuses on their wellbeing and wellness and that is the sole explanation of joining gyms, and here we can agree with their statement, but we also conclude that not every single one, but most of the gym freaks indulge into daily smoking and drinking, build an excellent body shapes by injecting various steroids, why do they do that? Are they really body and health conscious?

Straightforward response it's essentially an appearance off monstrosities, rather than being healthy, assuming that wellbeing was the overall subject and saying for them they would have done regular exercise from a beginning phase with ordinary yoga. How many gym freaks have you seen now and earlier in a yoga centre? Where were they, when yoga became popular didn't they care about their health and fitness?

Same applies for those riches (here rich not only means a billionaire, but also every single persons who has a little to excessive wealth) who have an egoistic proudness of one's wealth, by claiming a little piece of gold, they are so overpower through pride that they didn't even consider mediocre individuals as humans.

But there are other individuals who are completely different, who has tons and huge loads of abundance like Tata who doesn't have any bad egoistic attitude, in the wake of having immense supplies of abundance, still Mr Tata is one of the modest people on earth, who gives 60% of his organization's benefits to noble cause. This is the sort of abundance and affluent individual we really want in our society from everybody, the most elevated richness is the affluence in total agreement.

Egoistic prideness, is one of some unacceptable and most terrible perspectives that we ought to stay away from, being haughty and claiming yourself unrivalled to others destructs you. You will not be able to appreciate others success, talents and achievements because for you these things can be done perfectly, when you are the doer and when you see others doing above and ahead of you, others achievements and accomplishments are more noteworthy than you, you became envious and develop envy towards them, you started to hate them for absolutely **no reason** at all, may be you don't even know them personally still you hate them, and the reason for the *hatred* is that you cannot *tolerate their success and achievements.*

These *attitude* of yours will eventually be *fatal* for you, just because you got *success* in a particular field today *doesn't means you will be right in every aspect of life.* Most of the people consider popular celebrity to be their indirect mentor or guide, not just they follow them indiscriminately, they follow them in each and every part of their life. What the hell is that? Just because a person is a renowned artist, a famous actor or a famous sportsperson *doesn't mean everything he speaks towards life is meant to be true,* man if you really want to learn something from that person, only listen to, what he speaks in his respective field, where he got his success. ***Your life's mentor and guide can only be your parents, not any celebrity and certainly not any social media influencer.***

CHAPTER NINETEEN

YOU ARE TAKING EVERYTHING FOR GRANTED.

Being less grateful for the things we have, is nothing less than a trend, that we are engaging in our day to day life. Right from getting up from the bed we continually contemplate the things that we don't have and being less grateful towards the things that we have. This negative mentality of our own, is continually making, a backhanded aggravation to us. It is totally **OK** to get the materialistic things that we want, however having said that, it is additionally our obligation to be somewhat keen to the things that we as of now have with us today.

Have you at any point look yourself in the mirror and express gratitude towards God, for the lovely body he gave it to you? Have you at any point been thankful in light of the fact that you are able to talk, to walk, to see, to hear? Perhaps not, because you have taken every little thing, that you have, for granted.

When you walk, it might not be a big task for you, sometimes you may even skip your task just because you have to walk a significant distance. This is the disposition that one needs to change. Ponder the individual, who can barely walk, contemplate the debilitated one, who is crippled. What sort of delight, he will be in if he could walk to even a bare distance. What sort of blissfulness will be for a deaf who could hear, for a moronic who could talk, for a visually impaired who could have seen the various shades of the nature and our general surroundings.

Meanwhile, you are stressing on the grounds that you don't have a rolex to wear? What about the one who doesn't have a hand? You are not satisfied by your looks just because somebody called you ugly or you disdain the shade of your skin? What about the one who doesn't have the ability to differentiate any colour, the only colour he has seen throughout his life is **black**? Still you think your aggravation is a lot of predominant? What's more important is to take a gander at your delightful body and thank the all-powerful for what you have and be somewhat appreciative.

You show your disinterest to eat in the event that you doesn't have your piece of chicken in your dinner? A festival without your beloved dish is less appreciable by you. According to the UN report on world hunger, 821million individuals, that is one in each nine individuals on earth doesn't have an appropriate meal to eat.

The assets of the world are enough for the world yet the ravenousness isn't. Have a legitimate look of things that you have, on your home, right from your furnishings, where you sit and take rest, to the music speakers that you play, to getting training, to wearing garments, to your devices, to your talents haven't you felt grateful for having them?

Have you at any point, felt granted that you can say and feel the words 'Maa' and 'Papa'? At any point, did you gander at your folks and be appreciative for having them in your day to day existence. A huge number of kids all over the world are vagrants. They have grown up living in a foster, you haven't. Your folks are whom you can entrust your existence with, the justification for your grin could not really be them however the justification for their grin is certainly you. The time you went out in the road, all that matters is the observation that you have towards different peoples living in the society, you will find men carrying heavy weighted goods in their shoulder ,only for their survival, you are having a way easier life then them, still you don't want to **improve ,upgrade** or **change** yourself.

You have underestimated everything, that is likewise one of the justification for why you don't get the things, which you need now. You could have failed to remember those occasions during the pandemic, when you were at your home caught up with making your favourite dalgona, which was simply done not to satisfy yourself, but to show and catch attention of others, however there were a many unfortunate families who were making a trip miles barefooted in order to reach their homes, this is the bitter truth of this toxic world, the cruel things that you overlook. Be thankful, that you are enjoying with your family in the that time, where numerous families weren't. Be *less worried* about *the things* that you *don't have*, they *don't guarantee happiness* even if you get or *achieve* them. Life is all about *searching happiness* in the things that you *already have.*

Every individual on earth, doesn't have all the things that they desire for, however we should be enough grateful for the things that we have today, because the things that *we have now* are also the things that someone else is *craving for their future.*

CHAPTER TWENTY

TAKE CARE OF YOUR PARENTS

God decided to create your parents, because he himself cannot be present with you in its absolute form. From the day you are born to the day you will leave this very planet, you have the greatest liability towards your parents. Right from very beginning , they have fulfilled every single desire that you have requested, even at the *cost of their expenses.* Today we spend a hell lot of time in wasting and doing unnecessary stuffs by being on the internet, but rarely we have any time left for our parents.

You think your birthday is special because you were born? No, absolutely not, your birthday is special because that was the day when your mother was free from the physical pain that she had carried for months, *just to have you.* When we have started to crawl and walk for the first time, our parents were the ones who was there with us every minute, the moment we lose our balance, we never fall because they were the ones who were ready to *hold us.* Even throughout our life, when we fail in our difficult times, they were always there for us. They always motivates us in our difficult times. Because they are the only one on earth, who *never* in a thousand dreams wants us to suffer.They will *happily* be on the *losing end,* if we were to be crowned as the *winner.* They will easily forget their tears if they can *see us smile.* Various life examples were there where a father sells of his land, works extra hours, a mothers decide to work as a maid in some else house, she sells of his garments so that you live a life filled with happiness without any sort of difficulty. Such are the sacrifices that they make for us.

But what does the present people do now? As soon as they see their parents gets old, they think of them as an extra burden and literally abandons them. The increase number of abandon homes for the old, gives us an idea about what kind of humans we are evolving into. When you were young, you were never a burden for your parents then why are you having this evil mentality of thinking them as burden? Try to change this thought of yours, *your parents can never be your burden.* The only thing they need at the end phases of their life, is *your love and affection. Don't betray* and take away this *love* from them because the day you betray them, this betrayal will also *leads you* to day when your own children will *do the same with you.*

The beginning.....